Who Will Bell the Cat?

Retold and dramatised from the
Aesop's fable as a reading play
for partners or small groups.

Ellie Hallett

Ways to read this story

This story is suitable for school and home. Some 'how to read' ideas are below.

- With a partner or small group, take it in turns to read the rows.

- Don't rush! This helps you to say each word clearly.

- Think of yourselves as actors by adding lots of facial and vocal expression. Small gaps of silence also create dramatic energy. These techniques will bring the story to life.

- If you meet a new word, try to break it down and then say it again. If you have any problems, ask your teacher or a reading buddy.

- Don't be scared of unusual words. They will become your new best friends.
  (New words strengthen your general knowledge and enable you to become vocabulary-rich in your day-to-day life.)

Have fun!

'Run for it!'

'Oh no. Not again!'

'Here she comes!'

'Meow. Sniff, sniff. Meow.'

'Stop eating and start running,
Martha Mouse!'

'Cora the Cat is on the prowl again, and she's looking for us.'

'Emergency!
Scamper or be eaten, mice!'

'Quick, everyone!
Into the broom cupboard!'

'I hate the broom cupboard!'

'Get in and stop fussing, Morgan Mouse.'

'Pull your tail in, Morrie Mouse, and stop squeaking!'

'My tail *is* in. Stop pestering me.'

'Achoo!'

'Meow, sniff, sniff.'

'All in, so lie low, mice, and stay still! I said *stay still*!'

'Ah-choo!'

'This broom cupboard is full of dust.'

'It's also full of mice, Mary Mouse.'

'And it's very dark.'

'Ah-choo!'

'Move over, Mippy Mouse. You're squashing me to bits.'

'Purr, purr, meow.'

'Be quiet, everyone! Cora is having a cat nap on the other side of the broom cupboard door.'

'And she is waiting for us to come out, and then she'll grab one of us with her great big feet.'

'I said *be quiet*.

We need to be as quiet as mice, if that is at all possible.'

'Shh. Why is that engine running?'

'It's not an engine, Milly Mouse.'

'That's Cora the Cat purring because she's happy.'

'Why is Cora the Cat happy, Moppy Mouse?'

'It's because she thinks she's going to have a mouse for dinner.'

'A mouse for dinner? But I'm a ...'

'Oh for crying out loud!
I can't explain all that now, Milly, and please stop scratching.'

'But I like scratching! It gives me comfort.'

'Cora! Here, puss, puss, puss.'

'At long last Cora has been called to the kitchen by her human.'

'What's happening, Morris Mouse? Are we still in danger?'

'No, we're safe for the moment. Cora has gone off to have her cold dinner out of a tin.'

'Listen up, everyone. Master Mouse wants to speak.'

'Thank you, Morrie Mouse. I want to call a Mice Meeting to work out how to get rid of Cora the Cat.'

'A what? A nice meeting?'

'No, a *Mice Meeting*, Martin Mouse.'

'Why do we need a Mice Meeting?'

'To work out a way to get rid of Cora the Cat, of course!'

'Be in the pantry in five minutes, mice. And don't be late!'

'All clear. Everybody out. Achoo!'

(brief intermission to show that time is passing)

'Order! Quiet, everyone!

Are we all here?'

'Everyone present and correct,

Master Mouse.'

'I hope this Mice Meeting is going

to be nice and short.

I have things to do at home.'

'So do I, and I'm also getting

rather hungry.'

'Me too. What are you having for

lunch, Morrie Mouse?'

'Some fresh wheat seeds and a small piece of rind of cheese. How about you? What do you have ...'

'Qui-et! Or-der!'

'I announce that the Meeting of the Mice is now open.'

'Stop talking and start thinking!'

'We are here to discuss the serious problem of Cora the Cat and how we can stop her trying to eat us.'

'I don't like being scared day in, day out.'

'I'm very stressed and that's a fact.'

'Me too. My eyebrows are turning white with worry.'

'Ahem ... Attention everyone.

We all know that Cora the Cat is a very big pest.'

'I hate her big staring eyes!'

'I'm scared of her long swishy tail!'

'It's her twitching whiskers that bother me!'

'I don't like her big fat furry feet.'

'Worse than that – she has sharp claws in her big fat furry feet.'

'But, but, but – what about her horrible huge and hungry teeth!'

'The worst thing is the sound of her loud sniffing when she's hunting for a mouse snack.'

'Quiet! Order! We need a lot less chat and many more ideas otherwise we will get nowhere!'

'I agree. We need an action plan and we need it now.'

'What's an action plan?'

'I've never heard of an action man! That could be a very handy thing to have. Yes, I like it!'

'Not a man. A *plan*! We need an action plan to get rid of Cora the Cat.'

(pause to show that the mice are thinking)

'Yes! I have it! We can jump on her tail to stop her walking!'

'That's a silly idea!'

'Um ... We can, um ...'

'We can tie her up when she's asleep!'

'That's an even sillier idea!'

'We can put flour on her dinner.'

'I can't believe what I am hearing!'

'What about biting all her fur off?'

'Yuk! Far too dry and hairy!'

'Think, mice, think!'

(pause)

'Well ... How about we put a jingly jangly bell around her neck.'

'How does a jingly jangly bell around her neck work?'

'When the bell rings ding-a-ling, we will know that Cora the Cat is on her way to catch one of us!'

'Now we're talking!'

'At last - a clever action plan.'

'A bell!

Around her neck! Now that's what I call smart thinking!'

'Brilliant!'

'Fantastic!'

'Around her neck, you say?'

'Yes oh yes. A great big bell around Cora's great big neck that rings loudly!'

'Wow and double wow! This idea is both fantastic and brilliant.'

'Paws up if you vote yes for the idea to bell the cat.'

'Yes.' 'Yes.' 'Yes!' 'Yes.' 'Yes.'

'Carried! Every mouse in this house has agreed with this action plan to bell the cat.'

'Um ... um ... What action plan?'

'Don't you ever listen, Michael Mouse?

The vote was carried to bell the cat!'

(short pause)

'Um ... but ...'

'What is it *now*, Michael Mouse?'

'Um ... well ... I can see a problem with this action plan.'

'Oh, for goodness sake! What sort of problem?'

'Um ... Who will bell the cat? What is the, um, action plan for making this action plan work?'

'I am more than happy to take it on. Oops. Maybe not. I have just remembered something.'

'Sorry. Can't do it either. Lots of jobs at home. Must go.'

'My babies are hungry.

See you later.'

'I have an appointment for a whisker trim.'

'Oh goodness me! Is that the time? Must fly!'

'Stop, mice! Stay where you are.'

'You all voted *Yes* to bell the cat.'

'We will now vote for who will carry out the plan.'

'No.' '*No.*' 'No.' 'Not me.' 'No way!'

'I have a sore leg.'

'I have an earache!'

'I have toothache.'

'I have a bad back.'

'I have a *very* bad back *and* an earache.'

'Oooo. My head! I must go home and lie down at once.'

'I think I am going to faint ...'

'Or-der!
I have reached the conclusion that a good idea is only good if it can be carried out.'

'You've hit the nail on the head, Master Mouse. Our plan was good, and then it was not good.'

(pause)
'Oh no! Big staring eyes!'
'Long swishy tail!'
'Twitching whiskers!'
'Big fat furry feet!'
'Huge claws in big fat furry feet!'
'Horrible huge hungry teeth!'
'Emergency! Emergency!'
'Cora is just around the corner!'
'Run for your life!'

(pause)

'Sniff, sniff, meee-oooow.'

'That's funny! I'm sure I heard some nicy-micy snacks squeaking near here.'

(all readers make a long meow and then pretend to sniff the audience/surroundings for mice)

'Meow! Purr.'

(readers share this speech)

And the moral of this Aesop's fable is that a plan will only work if it can be carried out.